SARAH NOLAN-QUINNEY   -   THE RAW FOOD MUM

RAW FOOD
4 KIDS™

In dedication to...

Hamish, Issy and Mum

To the love of my life and best friend Hamish, who first introduced me to raw foods with bananas and chocolate sauce on our first date. You continue to support and encourage me in ways that I never expected. I'm so happy to be growing young with you. I wove you Bubba x

To my beautiful daughter Isabelle who inspires and teaches me something new every day. I cherish every single moment with you darling. You have helped me be the person I wanted to be, your mum. I love you more than anything in the whole universe. You are my little raw of sunshine baby girl x

My Mum. I love you Mum! You are my everything. I am so lucky and blessed to call you my mum! I hope I am the Mum to Issy that you are and have been to me. You are my rock, your are my world, I love you x

'Let food be
thy medicine
and medicine
be thy food'

welcome...

I am so thrilled you want to start making yummy raw, healthy, live, nutrient dense food for your little ones and your family!

Hamish and I have been thriving on a love of raw live food since 2008 and as a mum to a beautiful raw food loving daughter Isabelle, I know first hand the benefits of raw food in a child's diet.

I feel blessed that I have gained so much knowledge about the raw food lifestyle that I am now able to share this with you through my book Raw Food 4 Kids.

This book is designed for those who want to start eating raw food but do not know where to start. The recipes are what I call raw versions of popular conventional recipes that children and adults know and love - making the transition that little bit easier!

I hope you find Raw Food 4 Kids to be a refreshing look at raw food for the whole family. Proving raw food can be fun, easy to prepare, creative, nutritious and most importantly it is food that the whole family can enjoy!

Sarah x

contents...

EVERY RECIPE IS 100% RAW

Snacks cont...

- Mesquite balls
- Chocolate chia balls
- Apricot balls
- Teddy bear biscuits
- Fruit roll ups
- Sweet potato chips
- Apple goji bars
- Apple cookies
- Muesli bars
- All seed bar

Crackers & Breads...

- Honey buns
- Veggie crackers
- Raw bread and variations
- Banana crackers
- Flaxseed bread
- Zucchini wraps
- Coconut wraps

Milk & Butter & Yoghurt...

- Almond butter
- Almond milk
- Sunflower milk
- Coconut yoghurt

Cheese & Creams...

- Raw cheese
- Cheese sticks
- Tahini cream
- Nut cream
- Sunflower seed dip

Preservative, Additive & Dairy Free

Sweets & Treats...

- Banana muffins
- Banana cream
- Ice cream and toppings
- Raw popcorn
- Chocolate mousse
- Mini cheese cakes
- Chocolate brownies
- Chocolate crackles
- Raw chocolate
- Juice cake

Resources...

- Pantry essentials
- Conversion chart
- Substitution chart
- Meal planner
- Kitchen essentials
- About The Raw Food Mum

Let food be
thy medicine
and medicine
be thy food

LET'S GET STARTED...

What is Raw Food?

Raw food is food that has not been heated above 115 degrees Fahrenheit or 46 degrees Celsius.

Raw foods include;

- All raw fruits and vegetables
- Nuts and seeds
- Sprouts
- Fresh herbs and raw spices
- Super foods
- Seaweeds
- Cold pressed oils

The standard Australian diet of both children and adults currently consists of large quantities of protein meats, processed sugars, high fat, processed dairy, flour products, most cooked grains, candy, soda, coffee, alcohol, chemicals, additives, preservatives, drugs, the list goes on and on.

A raw food diet has benefits for everyone in the family. Eating lots of raw food can make a huge difference in your families energy, health, weight, mood, and quality of life. The human body requires enzymes to digest food. Each whole raw food contains naturally occurring enzymes designed to help break down that particular food. Cooked foods above 115 degrees Fahrenheit/ 46 degrees Celsius start to loose these enzymes, nutrients, minerals and vitamins. Essentially eating cooked foods is like eating empty calories.

Organically grown raw and living foods provide high-quality nutrition while naturally supporting both proper digestion and a well-functioning immune system. With raw food, digestion and elimination are quick and easy. Eating raw live foods helps to alkalize the body, a key factor in building excellent health. When the body is in an alkaline state, it is better able both to absorb nutrients and expel toxins more efficiently. When you have an alkaline body you have a healthy body and then you have healthy children.

Most people know it is healthy to eat fresh, fruits and vegetables especially when it comes to feeding our children. What many people don't know is that you can feed your children raw food. Raw food is perfectly designed for our children's growing bodies and you can also feed your children raw foods from an early age, in fact the earlier the better!

Why Raw Food for Kids?

These statistics are just plain scary! Something has to change...

- 8% of Australian children are obese[1]

- 17% of Australian children are over weight[2]

- 1/3 of Australian children consume little or no fruit or vegetables[3]

- 78% of Australian children don't meet the dietary guidelines for daily vegetable intake[4]

- 39% of Australian children don't meet the guidelines for daily fruit intake[5]

- There is a general decline in fruit consumption in Australian children between 2 – 11 years of age[6]

- 32% of Australian mums find it difficult to get their kids to eat fruit in their school lunches[7]

With these alarming statistics I feel it is so important to start improving the health of our children. Where does this start? I feel it starts in the home, by replacing all processed and packaged foods, start by including whole and raw live foods as much as you can.

With the growing rate of disease, learning disabilities and obesity in our children it is becoming even more important to wind the clock back and start feeding our children "REAL FOOD", not the processed packaged food that is simply designed to make profits not nourish our children.

Organically grown raw and raw living foods provide high-quality nutrients while naturally supporting both proper digestion and a well-functioning immune systems. When children eat these life-giving foods it helps to alkalize their bodies, a key factor in building excellent health and immunity.

"As parents we have a responsibility to set an example and teach our children what REAL food is! Let's make our kids proud"

1-2: Productivity Commission Report Childhood Obesity: an Economic Perspective. 3: 'School Child Nutrition', prepared by the Department of Nutrition and Food Services Royal Children's Hospital, Published by the Public Health Group, Victorian Department of Human Services. 4-5: Australian National Children's Nutrition and Physical Activity Survey 2007 6: 'School Child Nutrition', prepared by the Department of Nutrition and Food Services Royal Children's Hospital, Published by the Public Health Group, Victorian Department of Human Services 7 Naturo Research Study, conducted by motherinc.com.au

When food is cooked, it looses at least 30% of the nutrients and 100% of the enzymes.

If you don't have enough enzymes, the body doesn't have the energy to develop new cells, fight off infections, or digest your food. By feeding your children raw foods, they are literally being fed living energy!

Nutrients are the building blocks of cells in our bodies and enzymes aid digestion and other bodily functions. Raw Foods are packed full of nutrients and enzymes perfect for growing kids!

Raising a Raw family...

I really want to stress that when it comes to children; it is not about being 100% raw, it is about including more raw live food in their diet and your families diet. That might be one raw meal a day or by making all your snacks raw. It is about including a percentage of raw food that works for YOUR family.

What is 100% Raw?

When you go 100% raw, people can experience great benefits soon after they go raw, almost an enlightenment feeling. Hamish went 100% raw overnight – he threw out any and all cooked food in the house. I on the other hand made a slower transition to raw. It took me about 2 months to go 100% raw. I had a green smoothie everyday then I started to crave more raw. I progressed to a raw lunch, then I slowly switched to a raw dinner. Before I knew it, I was eating a 100% raw vegan diet.

What is High Raw?

The definition of high raw is consuming between 80%-95% of raw foods. What this means is that people who are high raw intend to eat raw all of the time, but in certain situations they are a little more flexible. For example, when eating out with family and friends and a restaurant does not have a raw food option we will eat a vegetarian or vegan meal. It is about being flexible but knowing that when you get home you will get straight back to eating raw food. This is where we sit. Even though we might be 100% at some stages our lives, I can never truly say we are 100% raw, but I do know the benefits my body experiences eating at this level. We do choose to eat fully raw in our home though, and balance with a vegan meal when out if there is no raw option.

One or Two Raw Meals a day option

This is the most common method for increasing your raw food intake. The idea is to make one of your daily meals raw. It may be your breakfast, lunch or dinner. With children you may replace all snacks with raw food snacks, or include a green smoothie in their daily diet. This is a great method for including raw food into your families diet, without placing to many expectations too early in your raw food journey.

DO I Recommend ~~going 100%~~ RAW?

When deciding to go 100% raw and if staying raw for a period of time, it is not only the food that changes in your life, the people, the social, the spiritual, the way you look at the world will change.

For an adult if you want to be 100% raw, I say YES go for it. Whatever amount of raw food you eat, your body, mind and spirit will thank you for it. You will feel alive, vibrant, light and energetic. Health aliments and disease will disappear when eating a 100% raw diet. However, what works for one person or family doesn't necessarily work for another. I feel It is really important to stress that any percentage of raw food in your child's and family's diet is going to benefit your health, of course the higher the percentage the better the results.

DO I believe children should be raised on a 100% Raw diet?

Isabelle, is fed a VERY high raw food diet, however she is not 100% raw. For most raising a child on a 100% raw vegan diet is simply not achievable for many reasons including; social, financial, time, availability of produce, school setting, peer pressure to name a few. There are only a handful of families in the world, that I am aware of that are raising 100% raw vegan children.

I initially wanted to raise Issy as a 100% raw vegan child, however after much research, I feel nature offers us certain nutrients through animal by products for certain stages in our developing life. And some foods for children are best cooked. It is tragic that animals are now being abused and kept in conditions that are of no benefit, other than to increase company profits. Please, when you purchase any animal meat or animal by products make sure you source them from a caring and sustainable farm.

So what does Issy eat? Issy is a vegetarian child, who eats a very large amount of raw foods. She eats a limited range of cooked foods such as quinoa, brown rice & steamed vegetables. The only animal product Issy eats sparingly are organic eggs, and organic goats cheese. Not only does she thrive on this diet, she naturally gravitates towards the raw foods.

Whether raising a child raw or not, I strongly believe that every parent has the choice to cut out processed, artificial, packaged, sugar laden foods from their child's diet. It is about being aware of the nutrient demands of a growing child, and making the right healthy choices for your family and your children.

Tips to eating raw...

Start your day with Fruit

Begin the day with fresh fruit for breakfast. Try a fresh fruit smoothie minus the dairy.

Transition to Raw

Transition raw foods into your regular cooked meals on a weekly basis. Or include some raw foods with your cooked family meals.

Green Smoothies

Get the family involved in green smoothies! Start off with a small amount of greens such as spinach or kale and slowly increase the amount of greens over time.

Experiment

Try using different food preparation techniques to add variety, such as sprouting seeds, grains, beans, juicing fruits and vegetables, soaking nuts and blending. Invest in a dehydrator.

Choose Organic

Be aware of the source of your food and purchase organic and local food where possible. Check the labels of any packaged foods for additives and preservatives.

Create Community

Join a local raw potluck or meet up group. It is a great way to meet people who share the same passion for raw food, share prepared food, exchange ideas and raw food recipes.

Raw Desserts

Learn to make raw food snacks and desserts. You don't need to abandon your sweet tooth; try transitioning conventional sweet foods to raw foods.

Snacking

Eat fresh fruit or raw vegetable sticks. Drink fresh powerful nutrient-packed green juices in between meals. Have a big fruit bowl on the kitchen bench! If your hungry simply eat a piece of fruit.

Cut out the Crap

Start by reducing or eliminating junk food, packaged snacks, fried foods, white sugar and white flour. Go into your cupboard and actually toss them out, or give them away.

Make Food Together

Get kids in the kitchen Kids love to be in the kitchen and it is a great place to start educating your children about fruits and vegetables, and the benefits of healthy choices!

Calcium Protein and Iron...

● Calcium

Calcium is an essential mineral and is crucial for heart function, muscle development, regulation of nerve tissue and blood vessel function as well as skeletal support.

Sources of calcium can be found in dark green leafy vegetables such as kale, broccoli, cabbage, parsley, watercress, seaweed, dried figs, dates along with nuts, almonds and brazil nuts.

High sources of calcium on a plant based diet include;

- Sesame seeds
- Tahini
- Chia seeds
- Almonds
- Leafy greens like kale
- Collard greens
- Seaweeds
- Kelp
- Dulse

● Iron

Iron is an essential nutrient because it is a central part of haemoglobin, which carries oxygen in the blood. Sources of iron include;

- Spinach
- Beet greens
- Sesame seeds
- Cashews
- Raisins
- Organic apricots
- Watermelon
- Kale
- Sunflower seeds
- Broccoli
- Pumpkin seeds
- Sun-dried tomatoes
- Seaweed
- Ground flax seed

⬤ Protein

Every food we eat contains protein. This includes all fruits, vegetables, nuts, seeds, legumes and grains. There is more than enough protein in the raw diet to satisfy the body's needs in sweet fruit, which averages 4 to 8% of calories of protein, and vegetables and leafy greens, which average 15 to 20% of calories of protein. Here are some excellent sources of protein.

Below is an overview of the (average) percentage of calories from protein

Sprouts > 55%
Green leafy vegetables > 35-50%
Nuts & seeds > 12-20%
Other vegetables > 10- 45%
Grains > 8-20%
Fruits > 1-10%

Leafy Green Vegetables

Dark green vegetables will serve your protein needs and provide your body with calcium, chlorophyll, vitamins, minerals and amino acids. Broccoli contains 45% protein. Spinach contains 30% protein. Two cups of kale provides 4 grams of protein.

Vegetables

Vegetables are a good source of protein on a raw diet, however you cannot meet your daily protein requirements with just vegetables. Eaten with fruit, leafy greens and a small amount of nuts and seeds, vegetables like carrots and celery will help supply enough protein to meet your needs.

Nuts & Seeds

Nuts and seeds are sources of good healthy fats and omega 3, 6 & 9's. Hemp seeds are the only food known to have a perfect harmony of omegas 3,6 and 9. They are also 22% protein. Pumpkin seeds are 21% protein. Almonds are 12% protein.

Alkaline v's Acidic...

There are two types of foods: acidic and alkalizing foods. Most raw foods and especially greens are alkaline forming in the body. Foods like sugar, meat, alcohol, cheese, and chocolate are very acidic. Acidity encourages decomposition, decay, disease and energy loss. The human body creates both acidity and alkalinity, but the standard Australian diet overloads our system with too much acidity. It is ok to have some acid foods in your diet a good percentage is 80% alkaline to 20% acid.

Alkaline foods support balance in the body. Green leafy vegetables, sprouts, and fresh fruits are all alkalizing. Our bodies need to be in an alkaline state to be healthy and blood cells need to remain at a constant pH of 7.3 (alkaline) to remain alive. What does all this mean? Well to encourage health in our children we need to be feeding them whole food, raw food and organic alkalizing foods. Disease can not thrive in an alkaline body - which is why people reverse disease on a raw food diet.

7.36 is the optimum pH for human blood

It takes 20 parts of alkalinity to neutralise 1 part acidity in the body

Consume alkaline foods freely! Most raw foods are alkaline forming

Most foods become more acidic when cooked

Alkaline PH

10.0

pH 9.5 alkaline water	Parsley	All sprouted beans
Himalayan salt	Broccoli	Sprouts
Grass	Sprouts	
Cucumber	Sea Vegetables	
Kale	Kelp	
Kelp	Green drinks	
Spinach		

9.0

Avocado	Ginger	Red onion
Beetroot	Green Beans	Tomato
Capsicum	Lettuce/ Rocket	Lemon/ Lime
Cabbage	Mustard greens	Butter beans
Celery	Okra	Beans
Collard/Spring greens	Onion	Chia seeds
Endive	Radish	Quinoa
Garlic		

8.0

Neutral PH

Artichokes	Watercress	Goat milk
Asparagus	Grapefruit	Almond milk
Brussels sprouts	Coconut	Most herbs &
Cauliflower/ Carrot	Buckwheat	Spices
Chives / Courgette/	Quinoa / Spelt	Avocado oil
Zucchini / Leeks	Lentils / Tofu	Coconut oil
Peas	Other Beans &	Flax Oil
Swede	Legumes	

7.0

Black Beans Chickpeas	Watermelon	Pecan nuts
Garbanzos /	Amaranth / Millet	Hazel nuts
Kidney Beans	Oats / Oatmeal	Sunflower oil
Cantaloupe /Currants	Rice	Grape seed oil
Fresh Dates / Nectarine	Hemp protein	
Plum	Freshwater	
Sweet Cherries	Brazil nuts	

6.0

Acidic PH

5.0

Ketchup	Orange	Wheat
Mayonnaise	Peach	Wholemeal bread
Butter	Pineapple	Wild rice
Apricot	Strawberry	Wholemeal pasta
Green bananas	Brown rice	Ocean fish
Mango	Oats	
Mangosteen	Rye bread	

4.0

Alcohol	Miso	Farmed fish
Coffee & Black tea Fruit	Rice syrup	Pork
Juice (Sweetened)	Soy sauce	Shellfish
Cocoa	Vinegar / Yeast	Cheese
Honey	Dried fruit	Dairy
Jam	Beef	Artificial sweeteners
Jelly	Chicken	Syrup
Mustard	Eggs	Mushrooms

3.0

What is dehydrating?

Dehydration is a method of food preservation that works by removing water from food, inhibiting the growth of bacteria. It has been practiced since ancient times to preserve food via natures sunshine! We now have electric dehydrators which can speed up the drying process and ensure more consistent results.

Important note when feeding children dehydrated foods

Dehydrated foods have lost their water content, so when feeding your children dehydrated foods it is important to ensure they drink lots of water. One of the main benefits of a raw food diet comes from eating water-rich foods that are easy to digest. Because dehydrated foods have lost their water content, it can be easy for children to overeat them. It is important to remember that children on a daily basis should be eating lots of fresh water rich fruits and vegetables and water.

So why is dehydrating not cooking?

During the dehydration process water is removed by evaporation. By keeping a consistent temperature of 115 degrees Fahrenheit / 46 degrees Celsius ensures the food is not cooked and bacteria, yeasts and mould which need water in the food to grow are prevented from surviving in the food. Cooking compared to dehydration kills the cellular and enzyme structure of food due to the extreme high temperatures and length of time which food is cooked.

Can you use an oven? I have been told that some recipes work using an oven on the lowest temperature setting with the oven door slightly ajar. I can't promise they will turn out raw - however it is still going to be a healthier option if you do not have dehydrator.

Temperature Control

To ensure that the enzyme structure of food is not damaged it is important to ensure that the temperature does not go above 115 degrees Fahrenheit / 46 degrees Celsius will ensure you keep the food in a raw state.

Why do you start the process at 145F/62C and then reduce it to 115F/46C? When you start the dehydration process, food contains a lot of moisture and stays quite cool. Starting at 145 degrees Fahrenheit helps the food remove the moisture quicker, it can also help ensure that food does not ferment. It is always important to decrease the temperature back to 115F/46C after one hour.

The Benefits of Sprouting...

Sprouts have always been a popular nutritious food. Sprouts like radish, alfalfa, clover, soybean, and broccoli are excellent sources of protein and offer a wide range of different nutrients that can help maintain good health. They are easy to sprout and are a great way to get the kids involved in growing food!

Sprout	Protein	Vitamins	Minerals
Alfalfa	35%	A, B, C, E, K	Calcium, Magnesium, Potassium, Iron, Zinc
Adzuki	25%	A, C, E	Iron, Niacin, Calcium
Buckwheat	15%	A, C, E	Calcium
Clover	30%	A, B, C, E	Calcium, Magnesium, Potassium, Iron, Zinc
Fenugreek	30%	A	Iron, Niacin, Calcium
Lentil	25%	A, B, C, E	Iron, Calcium, Phosphorus
Mung bean	20%	A, C, E	Iron, Potassium
Radish	Yes	C	Potassium
Sunflower	Yes	B Complex, E	Calcium, Iron, Phosphorus, Potassium, Magnesium
Wheat (and Rye)	15%	B Complex, C, E	Magnesium, Phosphorus

How to Sprout...

1. Cover sprouts in a jar with water, then place a muslin cloth on top with elastic band.

2. Rinse and drain your sprouts morning and night.

3. Always rinse your sprouts until the water is clear and drain.

4. Store your sprouts in a sealed container in the fridge.

Why Choose Organic?

When choosing organic foods from local, sustainable and organic farms you also support the larger community of which we are all a part of. Organic food is free of synthetic pesticides and fertilizers. By eating products raised on organic farms you provide the healthiest choice for your family and support the farms that support healthy ecological neighbourhoods.

Organic agriculture works for a healthy balance of the soil, using crop rotation and other techniques to help improve soil fertility instead of controlling the environment with chemicals. Look for these certified logos when purchasing organic food:

Nutrition
Organic foods and ingredients contain higher levels of vitamins, minerals and health-promoting antioxidants.

The Planet
Approximately 1/3 of the average consumer's carbon footprint comes from the contents of their grocery cart. This number could be significantly reduced by choosing organic foods.

Our Wildlife
Chemicals and pesticides used in non-organic farming practices pose a significant threat to many species of wildlife, imagine what these chemicals do to the gut of a child.

GMO Free
While we still lack a complete understanding of the impacts of consuming genetically modified ingredients. There is evidence that it could lead to the creation of new diseases, nutritional problems and unpredictable side effects including allergies. I personally feel it is important to exclude any GMO foods from a child's diet.

What is The Dirty Dozen?

If you can't always source organic food, below is the 'Dirty Dozen List'. You can lower your pesticide intake by avoiding the 12 most contaminated foods listed as the Dirty Dozen or choosing the least contaminated produce listed as the clean 15.

The Dirty Dozen:

Buying organic versions of the following from local farmers markets, or home grown whenever possible are the best options for the following foods;

- Apples
- Celery
- Sweet bell peppers
- Peaches
- Strawberries
- Imported nectarines
- Grapes
- Spinach
- Lettuce
- Cucumbers
- Blueberries
- Potatoes
- Green beans
- Kale, collards, and leafy greens

The Clean 15:

Conventionally grown items on the "Clean 15" list are generally low in pesticides these include;

- Onions
- Sweet corn
- Pineapple
- Avocado
- Cabbage
- Sweet peas
- Asparagus
- Mangoes
- Eggplant
- Kiwi
- Cantaloupe
- Sweet potatoes
- Grapefruit
- Watermelon
- Mushrooms

Age Chart & Super food Benefits...

I have carefully selected a range of superfoods foods that I believe provide the maximum amount of nutrition per serving for your growing child. The best part about superfoods is that they are foods in their purest state, minimally processed if at all.

When introducing food for the first time always ensure you do the four day wait rule, so if your child has an adverse reaction to a new food, you will have just a few foods to look to as the culprit. Always ensure you read and follow the package for serving sizes for each age. The appropriate age of introduction is listed next to the food title.

Spirulina 7m+

Spirulina contains rich protein 3~4 times higher than fish or beef. Vitamin B12 is 3~4 times higher than animal liver, as well as iron, potassium, magnesium sodium, phosphorus, calcium etc. With over 100 nutrients, Spirulina is often described as the most complete food source in the world.

Raw Honey 12m+

Raw honey has anti-viral, anti-bacterial, and anti-fungal properties. It promotes body and digestive health and is a powerful antioxidant. It strengthens the immune system, eliminates allergies, and is an excellent remedy for skin wounds and infections.

Flaxseeds 7m+

High in most of the B vitamins, magnesium, and manganese, this little guy is also packed full of omega-3 fatty acids which are important for brain development. Freshly ground, they are a very good source of soluble fibre.

Goji Berries 12m+

Unique among fruits because goji berries contain all essential amino acids, they have the highest concentration of protein of any fruit. They are also loaded with vitamin C, have twenty-one trace minerals, and are high in fibre. Boast 15 times the amount of iron found in spinach, as well as calcium, zinc, selenium and many other important trace minerals, there is no doubt that the humble goji berry is a nutritional powerhouse.

Chia Seeds 8m+

These little guys are worth their weight in gold. They are high in fibre, omegas, calcium, protein & antioxidants. Adding just two tablespoons of chia seeds to your daily diet will give you approximately seven grams of fibre, four grams of protein, 205 milligrams of calcium, and five grams of omega-3. Chia has a neutral flavour, so it goes with just about anything.

Tahini 12m+

Is rich in minerals such as phosphorus, lecithin, magnesium, potassium and iron. It is one of the best sources of calcium out there, just 35 grams of tahini contains almost 35% of your recommended daily calcium intake. It also contains vitamin E and vitamins B1, B2, B3, B5 and B15.

Bee Pollen 12m+

Bee pollen is a complete food and contains many elements that products of animal origin do not possess. Bee pollen is more rich in proteins than any animal source. It contains more amino acids than beef, eggs, or cheese of equal weight. About half of its protein is in the form of free amino acids that are ready to be used directly by the body.

Cacao Powder 12m+

With more antioxidant flavonoids than any other food tested thus far, raw cacao powder makes a tasty and nutritious addition to any smoothie & energy bars. Cacao is made from the cacao bean, which in its natural state contains plenty of essential minerals like calcium and magnesium,

Coconut Water 8m+

Coconut water is the purest liquid next to water. It is isotonic which means that it easily slides into the body's cells to hydrate and nourish. Coconut water contains potassium, magnesium, other vitamins, and minerals that will help small (and big) bodies stay in a nutritionally balanced state.

Wheat Grass 12m+

Wheat grass has nearly a gram of protein per teaspoon. It provides eight of the essential amino acids, and thirteen of the nonessential amino acids. It contains Vitamins A, B1, 2, 3, 5, 6, 8, and 12; C, E and K, as well as 15mg of Calcium, 8mcg Iodine, 3.5mcg Selenium, 870mcg Iron, 62mcg Zinc, and many other minerals. Start with small amounts for little ones and dilute with water.

Nutritional Yeast 6m+

High in B vitamins and not to be confused with brewer's yeast, nutritional yeast is a flaked powder that is high in B12 and has a cheesy flavour. It is a great source of 18 amino acids, protein, folic acid, biotin and other vitamins. It is also rich in 15 minerals including iron, magnesium, phosphorus, zinc, chromium, and selenium.

Mesquite Powder 8m+

Mesquite is high in protein, low on the glycemic index, and a good source of soluble fibre, meaning it digests relatively slowly and does not cause spikes in blood sugar. This gluten-free powder is also a good source of calcium, iron, lysine, manganese, zinc, and potassium. The powder has a sweet, caramel-like flavour, making it an excellent sweetener for smoothies, and desserts.

Maca Powder 12m+

Maca root is rich in B-vitamins, which are the energy vitamins. It is also vegetarian source of B-12. Maca helps balance and aids in the regulation of healthy hormone production. Use small amounts with young children. Great for adults.

Buckwheat 9m+

A great substitute for grains for people who are sensitive to wheat or other grains that contain protein glutens. Buckwheat is a very good source of manganese and a good source of magnesium, copper, and dietary fibre. Buckwheat has more protein than rice, wheat, millet or corn. It is also low GI.

Hemp Seeds 8m+

Hemp seeds contain all 10 essential amino acids. 3 Tablespoons of Hemp Seeds = 11 grams of protein. Hemp seeds contain a healthy anti-inflammatory 3:1 ratio of omega-6 to omega-3 fat. In addition, hemp seeds contain an especially beneficial type of omega-6 fat called GLA (gamma linolenic acid). GLA is a direct building block of good anti-inflammatory hormones. Research suggests it may be useful for problems like eczema, allergies and rheumatoid arthritis.

Camu Camu 12m+

Strengthening the immune system, promoting energy and vitality. Camu camu supports healthy levels of white blood cell formation. 1/2 teaspoon of camu camu powder provides more than 400% the daily value of vitamin C! It also supports the optimal function of the nervous system including eye and brain functions.

Acai Berry 12m+

This dark purple berry is one of the most antioxidant-rich foods in the world, it contains a unique blend of dietary fibre, healthy fats, and phytosterols that promote cardiovascular and digestive health, as well as a wide spectrum of amino acids and trace minerals.

Lacuma Powder 12m+

Using lacuma powder is an excellent way to get a boost of rich antioxidants and B vitamins. Lacuma has also long been said to aid in healing and speed up wound closure, as it has natural antibiotic, antimicrobial, and antifungal properties

Coconut Nectar 12m+

Coconut nectar contains 17 amino acids, as well as a host of minerals and vitamin B and C. With a glycemic index of 35 compared to organic sugar's 47, raw sugar's 65, and refined sugar's 80. It is great sugar alternative.

Chlorella 7m+

Chlorella is a fresh water, single-celled algae that grows in fresh water. Chlorella helps boosts the immune system and helps fight infection. It has been shown to increase the good bacteria in the gastrointestinal (GI) tract. Chlorella is rich in vitamins A, B1, B2, B6, B12, C and E.

Linseed Oil 6m+

Linseed oil is an excellent source of omega-3s: Just 1 teaspoon contains about 2.5 grams, equivalent to more than twice the amount most people get through their diets. It contains 50 percent omega 3s, almost twice as much as contained in fish oil. Because it comes from a plant source, it is perfect for vegetarian and vegan kids

Kelp 12m+

Kelp contains B vitamins, which are essential for cellular metabolism and provides the body with energy. It also contains vitamins C and E, which are both strong antioxidants and promotes blood vessel health. Minerals, such as calcium, boron and magnesium are plentiful in kelp. These are necessary for strong bones and normal muscle function.

Nutrient reference chart...

Nutrition is important for everyone, but especially important for children because it is directly linked to all aspects of their growth and development; factors which will have direct ties to their level of health as they grow into adults. Here is a summary of where you can obtain nutrients from in a plant based diet.

Fats

Essential fatty acids are essential for brain and nerve function.

- Flaxseed oil
- Flaxseeds
- Hemp seed oil
- Olive oil - do not cook with olive oil
- Green leafy vegetables
- Avocados
- Nuts – Almonds & hazelnuts
- Coconut oil is great for cooking with as well

CARBOHYDRATES

For energy. Use complex carbohydrates - avoid sugar and white flour!

- Whole grain rice
- Wholemeal bread
- Oats
- Sweet potatoes
- Beans & lentils
- Buckwheat
- Quinoa

FIBRE

Vital for health, keeps bowels healthy and regulates appetite.

- Whole grains
- Beans and lentils
- Fruits and vegetables
- Nuts and seeds
- Chia and linseeds

Protein

For growth and repair of body tissue.

- Beans and lentils
- Tempeh
- Whole grains
- Seeds
- Nuts
- Hummus
- Quinoa

Vitamin A

Powerful antioxidant, sight, bone, teeth growth and tissue repair.

- Carrots
- Spinach
- Capsicum
- Watercress
- Tomatoes
- Green leafy vegetables
- Dried apricots (organic)
- Mango

B GROUP - includes; B1, B2, B3, B6, Folic Acid.

B vitamins are water soluble and are best served steamed or raw. Important for energy, using fats and proteins. Also for cell growth and nervous system.

- Beans sprouts
- Sprouts
- Avocado
- Whole grains
- Nuts
- Mushrooms
- Bananas
- Oranges
- Yeast extract
- Beans and lentils
- Green leafy vegetables

B12

Used in nerve formation and cell production. Deficiency can lead to anaemia

- Fortified products
- Fortified cereals
- Yeast extract
- Eggs
- If you have a vegan child it is highly recommended to use a B12 supplement.

Vitamin C

Used to fight infection and heal wounds. Great antioxidant

- Green leafy vegetables
- Cabbage
- Broccoli
- Parsley
- Snow peas
- Oranges

- Black currant
- Kiwi fruit
- Mango
- Blackberry
- Strawberries
- Papaya
- Rock melon
- Camu camu

Vitamin D

Your body must have vitamin D to absorb calcium. Too little vitamin D results in soft bones in children and rickets.

- Natural sunlight
- Fortified cereals
- D2 is animal free
- Egg yolks
- A supplement may be used in winter.

Vitamin E

Antioxidant used to protect against disease. Tissue healing. Skin health.

- Olive oil
- Tomatoes
- Avocado
- Apples
- Carrot
- Nuts and seeds

Vitamin K

Energy use. Fights infection.
For blood clotting. Healthy bones.

- Green leafy vegetables
- Kelp
- Lettuce
- Broccoli
- Peas
- Lentils

Grain & Nut Soaking Chart

Sprouts have always been a popular nutritious food, they are live food at its best. Seeds, nuts, legumes and grains are best eaten when they have been sprouted as they all have enzyme inhibitors in them as a protection mechanism from the elements until the time to sprout. Sprouts like radish, alfalfa, clover, soybean, and broccoli are excellent sources of protein and offer a wide range of different nutrients that can help maintain good health.

Variety	Measure	Soak	Rinse	Harvest	Yield
Soft nuts	1/2cup	12hours	2xday	1-2days	3/4cup
Hard nuts	1/2cup	24hours	2xday	1-2days	3/4cup
Small seeds	1/4cup	8hours	2xday	6-10days	4 cups
Large seeds	1/2cup	12hours	2xday	1-2days	3/4cup
Grains	1/4cup	8hours	2xday	2-3days	3/4cup
Beans/Legumes	1/4cup	12hours	2xday	2-3days	3/4cup

Soft Nuts: Cashews, pecans, walnuts

Hard Nuts: Almonds, macadamia, brazil nuts, hazelnuts

Small Seeds: Alfalfa, radish, clover

Large Seeds: Sunflower, pumpkin, sesame

Grains: Buckwheat, kamut, rye

Beans & Legumes: Mung beans, adzuka beans, chickpeas, lentils

cacao and carob

I do not recommend cacao for little ones (8 years and under) I recommend using carob instead and you will see an option for this throughout the recipes.

I don't want to take away the benefits of Cacao as there are many however, cacao contains Theobromine which is considered to be a stimulant. It has an effect that is similar to caffeine and black tea. Although theobromine itself does not have caffeine, the stimulation of the heart and nervous system that it causes acts like a caffeine. It is why I do not recommend cacao for young children, instead simply opt for an organic carob.

Different types of chocolate contain different amounts of theobromine. In general, theobromine levels are higher in dark chocolates (approximately 10 g/kg) than in milk chocolates (1-5 g/kg). Higher quality chocolate tends to contain more theobromine than lower quality chocolate. Cocoa beans naturally contain approximately 300-1200 mg/ounce theobromine (note how variable this is!).

So when it comes to my recipes – it is simple when making them for your little ones simply swap the Cacao to Carob! And like any sweet, chocolate should always be a treat for little ones!

Benefits of Carob Include: - Always try and purchase an organic source of carob where you can.

Carobs are high in protein, contain essential vitamins and are a healthy alternative to most snack foods. Carobs are beneficial as they:

- Full of antioxidants and phytonutrients.Gallic acid provides anti-allergic, antiseptic and anti-bacterial benefits.
- Rich in insoluble fibre.
- Good source of vitamin E.
- Contain Thiamin (vitamin B), Riboflavin (vitamin B2), Niacin (vitamin A), alpha-tocopherol, and ergocalciferol (vitamin D2).
- High in potassium and magnesium.
- Gluten free.
- Caffeine free.
- 100% natural with no chemicals or preservatives.

Raw Food Recipes

smoothies & juices...

What is a green smoothie

5 reasons

smoothie time

Let's get juicing

Juicing combinations

storing juice

The Green smoothie...

A green smoothie is made by blending green raw leafy vegetables such as spinach, kale, swiss chard, collard greens, celery, parsley, with fruit, such as, bananas (frozen bananas make smoothies creamy), oranges, kiwis, apples, mangoes, pears, blueberries. Blend with water, coconut water or a nut milk.

Green drinks get their vibrant colour from chlorophyll, a nutrient-rich pigment found in all green leafy vegetables they oxygenate the blood and help boost energy levels and support the immune system.

To balance flavour and nutrition the typical ratio of a green smoothie is about 60% fruit to 40% leafy greens. Ensure you rotate your greens regularly.

5 Reasons to include green smoothies...

- When you add greens to your smoothies you are digesting the **highest alkaline-forming foods.** Smoothies are made using the whole fruit/vegetable, you also get all the fibre in your drink.

- **Highly nutritious**: Greens are full of vitamins A, K, D, and E, which are all fat-soluble.

- Green Smoothies are an easy way to include **raw live foods into your children's diet.** You might need to start with a higher proportion of fruit versus vegetables for example, 70/30 instead of the standard 60/40, until children get used to the flavours.

- **Greens are full of chlorophyll,** which purifies the blood, prevents tooth decay, aids in proper digestion, helps detoxify the liver, keeps the thyroid gland in balance, cleanses internal organs, enhances capillary function, supports hormones, decontaminates inorganic chemicals, and builds up red blood cell counts.

- **Improved clarity/concentration of the mind and improved health:** Many notice a clarity of mind when eating greens in their diet; which is so important for our growing and learning children.

Green smoothies Made simple...

1. Choose a type of Liquid
* Water
* Coconut water
* Almond milk

2. Choose a type of Green
* Kale
* Spinach
* Swiss chard
* Beet tops
* Spirulina

3. Choose your Fruit
* Banana
* Blueberries
* Orange
* Apple
* Pear
* Mango

3. Super Smoothie it...
* Chia seeds
* Hemp seeds
* Camu camu
* Bee pollen
* Maca powder
* Lacuma powder
* Flax seeds

1.2.3. Blend liquids and greens together, then add fruit and super smoothie it. Most of all ENJOY!

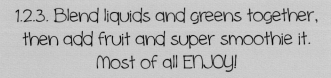

Issy's 1st Green smoothie...

Green smoothies are suitable from 9 months +

A simple first green smoothie...

Ingredients...
* 1/2 cup of spinach
* 1 frozen banana
* 1 ripe banana
* 1 cup of water

Method...
Blend greens and water first then add banana and blend until nice and creamy!

Ensure you rotate your greens reguarly!

smoothie time...

A healthy, homemade smoothie is the fastest and easiest way to feed your child their recommended daily servings of fruits and vegetables. Smoothies can easily provide your child with a full serving of fruit and vegetables – and all in just one cup!

Buy bananas in bulk when they are ripe and on sale! Cut them up into small pieces and into the freezer!

The best thing about smoothies for kids is...

- They are thirst quenching and satisfy hunger at the same time.

- They taste as bright and pretty as they look.

- They are a great way to sneak more fibre and antioxidants into your child's diet.

- They don't require a lot of fussy ingredients.

- They give new life to over ripe fruit.

- They can be easily tailored to suit individual needs. Even kids with dairy allergies can enjoy them.

- They are a great DIY snack for older kids and the whole family; younger operators will require adult supervision when using a blender.

smoothie ideas...

Banana Smoothie

1 ripe banana
1 frozen banana
1/4 cup of almond milk
1/4 teaspoon vanilla

Chocolate Milk

1 ripe banana
2 frozen bananas
1/2 cup of almond milk
2 Tablespoons of carob powder
2 dates

Berry Bliss

1 ripe banana
1 frozen banana
1/4 cup of almond milk
1/2 cup of frozen berries

Pineapple Delight

1 ripe banana
1 frozen Banana
1/2 cup of almond milk
1/2 cup of fresh pineapple
1 apple

Vanana Banana

1 ripe banana
1 frozen banana
1 teaspoon vanilla
1/4 cup of cashews
1 cup of almond milk

Orange Energy

1 ripe banana
1 frozen banana,
1 orange
1 cup of almond milk
2 Tablespoons of ground flaxseeds

Let's get Juicing...

Vegetable juice provides children with minerals, vitamins, essential fatty acids, enzymes, carbohydrates, proteins and more. When you include juices in your child's diet you will notice an increased energy, clarity of mind. Juicing will also help to support their developing immune system.

Juicing also allows you to consume an optimal amount of vegetables in an efficient manner. Juicing removes fibre which allows for the maximum amount of nutrients to reach a cellular level without having to go through the whole digestive process.

Some children simply don't like eating vegetables, but this can be easily overcome with a quick glass of vegetable juice, sweetened with some apple and lemon. It is important to add a variety of juices and blended foods in your child's diet for maximum nutrition. Get the kids involved when making juice.

Juice Ratios for little ones.

- 9 months: 1/4 juice & 3/4 water or coconut water
- 12 months: 1/2 juice & 1/2 water or coconut water
- 18 months: 3/4 juice & 1/4 water or coconut water
- 24 months: Juice and a dash of water or coconut water

Making your juice taste great.

- Add a higher percentage of sweet vegetables and fruit at the start of your juicing adventure and overtime increase the amount of greens.
- Lemons and Limes: You can also add a quarter to half a lemon or lime, leaving much of the white rind on.
- Fresh ginger: This is an excellent addition to juices in winter - if your little one can tolerate it.

Juicing Combinations...

Carrot Juice

Carrot & Apple
Spinach

Cucumber Juice

Cucumber
Parsley
Pear
Celery
Apples

Green Apple Juice

Apples
Cucumber
Spinach or
Kale
Lemon

Veggie Cleanser

Kale
Carrots
Celery
Apples
lemon

Beetroot Juice

Apples
Carrots
Beetroot
Lemon

How to store juice

Drinking your juice straight away is best to ensure oxidation does not occur. However here is a little trick if you want to make double the batch and store your juice for later or for the next day.

 1. Pour juice into a glass jar and fill it to the very top as close as you can to the lip of the jar.

 2. Place cling wrap, or canning jar seal over the top of the jar. We Re-use the plastic wrap that coconuts or vegetables come wrapped in, it is a great way of re-use, reduce and recycle.

 3. Screw the lid on over the top of the cling wrap or canning jar seal and refrigerate straight away. Juice will store for up to 48 hours refigerated.

 ## Using Cling Wrap

 ## Using Ball Mason Jars

Breakfast...

Chia seed pudding

simple Raw muesli

Buckwheat crunchies

Almond crumble

On the go bars

Pancakes

Chia seed pudding serves 2

ingredients

- 2 cups of almond milk
- 1/4 cup of chia seeds
- Sprinkle of organic sultanas
- Sprinkle of goji berries
- 2 drops of stevia (hazlenut stevia is great in this recipe)

method

- Place 1/4 cup of chia seeds, sultanas and goji berries with 2 cups of almond milk, stir and place into a container and seal.
- In one hour stir again to ensure all the chia seeds are absorbing the milk, and do not all sink to the bottom of the jar.
- Refrigerate over night.
- In the morning you have a very yummy chia seed pudding the kids will love.
- You can also add your favourite fruits and nuts to bulk it up! With Issy I often just add fruit and a sprinkle of LSA (ground linseed, almonds and sunflower seeds).

ROASTED MAPLE SALMON & BRUSSELS SPROUTS

Give your vegetables ample space on the baking sheet to ensure even roasting rather than steaming.

PREP TIME: 15 min.
TOTAL TIME: 45 min. **SERVES:** 4

¼ cup (60 mL) Sensations by Compliments Pure Maple Syrup

¼ cup (60 mL) canola oil

2 garlic cloves, minced

1 tbsp (15 mL) lemon juice

1 tbsp (15 mL) Sensations by Compliments Original Dijon Prepared Mustard

¼ tsp (1 mL) each salt and pepper

4 cups (1 L) Brussels sprouts, trimmed and halved

1 large red onion, halved and cut into wedges

½ cup (125 mL) Compliments Sultana Raisins

4 frozen Compliments Balance Wild Pacific Pink Salmon Fillets, thawed and patted dry

2 tbsp (30 mL) minced parsley

1 Preheat oven to 475°F (220°C).

The ultimate one-pot meal solution that does the cooking for you. Layer root vegetables on the bottom before placing your meat and liquid in the pot. Remember to add soft veggies or fresh herbs at the end to retain their flavour and texture.

on the
cover

A handy, nutritious and affordable protein fix.

LEMON-CAPER CHICKEN, POTATO & ASPARAGUS SKILLET

PREP TIME: 15 min. **TOTAL TIME:** 50 min. **SERVES:** 4

- 4 bone-in chicken thighs, skin removed
- ½ tsp (2 mL) each salt and pepper
- 2 tbsp (30 mL) canola oil, divided
- 1 onion, diced
- 3 garlic cloves, minced
- ¾ tsp (4 mL) fresh Compliments Thyme leaves
- 1 tbsp (15 mL) all-purpose flour
- ¾ cup (175 mL) Compliments Chicken Broth, 35% Less Sodium
- ¾ cup (175 mL) water
- 1 lemon, zested and juiced
- 1 tbsp (15 mL) capers, drained
- 12 Compliments White Petites Potatoes, halved
- 1 lb (500 g) asparagus, ends trimmed
- 2 tbsp (30 mL) minced parsley

1. Season chicken with salt and pepper. In a large deep skillet or Dutch oven, heat 1 tbsp (15 mL) oil over medium-high heat. Add chicken and cook, turning once, until golden brown, about 10 min. Transfer chicken to a plate and set aside.

2. Reduce heat to medium and return pan to heat. Add remaining oil to pan. Add onion, garlic and thyme and cook, stirring often, until softened and aromatic, about 5 min. Sprinkle with flour and cook, stirring, 1 min. Stir in chicken broth, water, lemon zest, lemon juice and capers and bring to a boil, scraping up any brown bits from bottom of pan. Add potatoes, cover, reduce heat to medium-low and cook, about 10 min.

3. Add chicken, bone side up, nestled amongst the potatoes. Cover and cook until potatoes are tender, about 20 min. Turn chicken over and lay asparagus over chicken and potatoes. Cover and cook until asparagus is tender, liquid is reduced and juices run clear when chicken is pierced, about 7 min. (or when an instant read thermometer inserted into the thickest part of the chicken, away from the bone, reads 165°F/74°C). Sprinkle with parsley.

PER SERVING (¼ OF THE RECIPE): 340 calories, 25 g protein, 16 g total fat (3 g sat. fat), 75 mg cholesterol, 23 g carbohydrates, 5 g fibre, 3 g sugars, 530 mg sodium

SKILLET

Why use lots of pans when you can use use just one? Brown meats and poultry first and then layer in the rest of your ingredients. Simmering everything together helps build flavour.

try it

simple raw muesli

ingredients

- 1 banana
- 1 apple
- 1/2 cup of nuts of choice; brazil, almonds, walnut etc..
- 1/4 cup of dates
- 1/4 cup of raisins
- Almond milk (see recipe 84)

Method

- Chop all ingredients into small pieces and mix well in a bowl.
- Serve with fresh almond milk (see recipe p.85)

BUCKWheat Crunchies

ingredients

- 4 cups of buckwheat
- 2 bananas
- 4 dates soaked in one cup of water
- 1 Tablespoon of super food powder i.e mesquite, maca, lacuma or camu camu.

Method

- Soak buckwheat overnight, rinse and drain.
- Place banana, dates and date water in a blender until smooth, adding your super food powder of choice.
- Mix the soaked buckwheat with the banana sauce, ensuring you cover the buckwheat evenly.
- Place mixture onto paraflex sheets and into your dehydrator on 115F/46C for 10-12 hours until nice and crunchy.
- Keep in a sealed container. Will last sealed for up to 2 months.
- Serve with almond milk and fresh fruit.

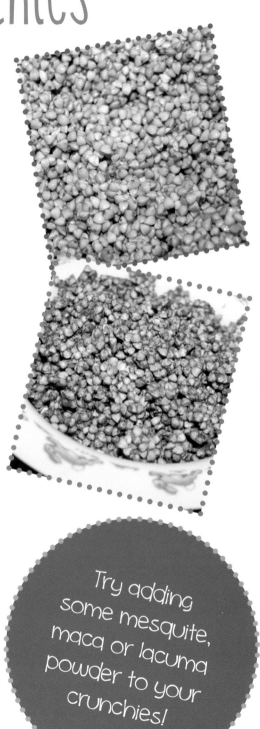

Try adding some mesquite, maca or lacuma powder to your crunchies!

ALMOND CRUMBLE

serves 2

Ingredients

- 4 cups of raw almonds soaked and peeled (see page 84 for details on how to peel almonds)
- 2 cups of coconut meat from young coconuts
- 1 Tablespoon of mesquite powder
- 1 teaspoon of Himalayan sea salt

Method

- Scoop 2 cups of coconut meat from young coconuts. (You can either drink the coconut water straight away or pour it into a glass jar and seal - will keep refrigerated for up to 4 days).
- Mix all the ingredients together in a food processor, until crumb like.
- Spread on dehdrator mesh trays evenly.
- Dehydrate at 145F/62C for 3 hours.
- Then reduce to 115F/46C for 4-5 hours or until nice and crunchy.
- Serve with fresh fruit, and nut milk.

Make sure to peel almonds as almond skins cannot be digested!

on the go bars makes 10-12

Ingredients

- 1 cup of raw almonds
- 2 Tablespoons of chia seeds
- 1 Tablespoon of mesquite powder
- 1 cup of desiccated coconut
- 1/2 cup of raisins chopped
- 1/2 cup of organic apricots chopped
- 1/2 cup of raw cacao nibs
- 1 teaspoon of cinnamon
- 4 Tablespoons of raw honey
- 3 Tablespoons of melted coconut oil
- 2 teaspoons of vanilla extract
- A pinch of Himalayan sea salt

Method

- Mix all dry ingredients in a food processor, until crumb like.
- Add liquid ingredients until mixture is sticky.
- Press mixture into a square tin.
- Sprinkle with coconut and cut into bars.
- Place in the fridge to set and store in refrigerator.

Chocolate banana pancakes

Makes 6-8

Ingredients

- 2 ripe bananas
- 1/3 cup of ground buckwheat
- 1/3 cup of ground flax seeds
- 1/3 cup of chia seeds
- 2 teaspoons of mesquite powder
- 3 teaspoons of cacao or carob powder
- 2 cups of almond milk
- 1 Tablespoon of coconut nectar
- A pinch of cinnamon

Method

- Mix all dry ingredients together in a high powered blender until fine.
- Add almond milk slowly until the mixture is batter like.
- Pour mixture onto a paraflex sheets forming pancake circles.
- Dehydrate at 145F/62C for 1 hour. Then reduce to 115F/46C for a further 4 hours, flip and continue to dehydrate for a further 4 hours.
- Serve with fresh fruit and raw banana cream - see recipe p95.

Lunch...

NORI ROLLS

veggie patties

Falafel's

vegetable soup

NORi ROLLS

Makes 4-6 long nori rolls

ingredients

- 1 packet of nori sheets (un roasted)
- 1/2 head of cauliflower
- 1/4 cup of raw cashews
- 1 Tablespoon of honey or coconut nectar
- 2 avocados skinned and sliced
- 1 cucumber cut into thin strips

Method

- Process cauliflower and cashews in a food processor until grainy in texture, add coconut nectar and pulse until combined.
- Lay nori sheet on chopping board.
- Cover 0.5cm of rice mixture over nori roll except 1cm of the outside edge facing away from you.
- Layer slices of vegetable down the centre and roll.
- Wet outside edge with water to stick, forming rolls!
- Cut into small pieces and serve.

vegetable suggestions

carrot
green onion
Avocado
cucumber
salad greens e.g.
spinach /lettuce
sweet bell pepper
mushroom
sprouts e.g. alfalfa,

veggie patties makes 8-12

ingredients

- 1 cup of walnuts
- 1/2 cup of hemp seeds
- 1/4 cup of ground flax seeds
- 3 cups of carrots chopped. You can also add any vegetable such as celery, parsley, tomato
- 1 medium red onion
- 2 cloves of garlic
- 1 teaspoon of Himalayan sea salt
- 1 Tablespoon of nutritional yeast
- 1/4 cup of filtered water

Method

- Combine all ingredients using a food processor, adding water slowly at the end.
- Process until well mixed but still with texture.
- Create pattie shapes and place on dehydrator mesh sheets.
- Dehydrate at 145F/62C for one hour.
- Continue dehydrating for 4-5 hours at 115F/46C or until they reach desired veggie burger consistency.

www.theorganicmum.com

Falafel

ingredients

- 2 cups of roughly chopped carrots
- 1 cup of sprouted chickpeas or 1 cup of dry sunflower seeds
- 2 sticks of celery
- 1/4 cup of ground flax seeds
- 1 cup of chopped fresh parsley
- 3 Tablespoons of diced brown onion
- 1 clove of minced garlic
- 1/4 teaspoon Himalayan sea salt
- 1/2 teaspoon cumin powder
- 1/2 cup of sesame seeds or hemp seeds to be used as the falafel crust

Method

- Place the chopped carrots into a food processor and process until fine.
- Add sunflower seeds or sprouted chickpeas, ground flax seeds, garlic, and spices and process until well mixed.
- Then add onions, parsley and celery and process further.
- Place all ingredients in a large bowl and roll into falafel balls. Coating the balls with hemp seeds or sesame seeds.
- Place onto paraflex sheets and dehydrate for 1 hour at 145F/62C and then for 4-6 hours at 115F/46C or until the outside becomes a little crispy! Serve warm or cold.

vegetable soup serves 2-4

ingredients

- 1/2 head of cauliflower or broccoli
- 3 medium zucchinis
- 1 parsnip
- 2 stalks of celery
- 1/2 cup of olive oil
- 1 teaspoon of finely chopped rosemary
- 6 tomatoes
- 2 avocados
- 1 teaspoon of Himalayan sea salt
- 1 Tablespoon of basil

Method

- Chop and marinate, cauliflower, zucchini, parsnip in olive oil and rosemary for at least 1 hour.
- Place marinated vegetables into the dehydrator for 2-3 hours at 115F/46C.
- Puree the tomato and avocado in a high powered blender until smooth.
- Place all pureed and dehydrated vegetables and remaining herbs into a pot warming the soup to 115F/46C.
- For the little ones, you can also blend all the ingredients to make a smooth soup instead of having the chunky vegetable pieces.

Dinner...

Pizza

Pasta

Lettuce Boats

Kids Salad

Raw Pizza

Makes 2 large pizza bases

Ingredients 4 base

- 1 cup of buckwheat
- 1 cup of cauliflower
- 1/2 cup of ground flax seeds
- 3/4 cups of fresh tomatoes or 1/4 cup sun-dried tomatoes
- 1/4 cup of olive oil
- 1/2 cup of brown onion
- 1 teaspoon Himalayan sea salt
- 2 teaspoons of coconut nectar
- 2 teaspoons of nutritional yeast
- 2 cloves of garlic

Method 4 base..

- Soak buckwheat for 12 hours, rinse and drain.
- Using a food processor, process buckwheat, cauliflower and ground flax seeds until crumb like, adding in all remaining ingredients and further processing until it forms a dough like consistency.
- Spread the mixture onto paraflex sheets, creating round or square pizza bases.
- Dehydrate at 145F/62C for 1 hour. Then further dehydrate at 115F/46C for 3-4 hours or until you can flip the crusts over and continue dehydrating a further 4-6 hours.

Raw Tomato Sauce

SAVE TIME!
Make and freeze crusts placing them back in the dehydrator when you are ready to make pizza!

- 3/4 cup of sun-dried tomatoes, soaked for 4-6 hours then drained
- 1-2 fresh tomatoes
- Handful of fresh basil
- 2-3 dates pitted
- A pinch of Himalayan sea salt
- A pinch of dried oregano and basil
- 1 1/2 teaspoons of olive oil
- Process all ingredients together in a high powered blender until smooth.

Method to assemble Pizza

- Spread tomato sauce mixture on dehydrated pizza bases.
- Place vegetables such as mushroom, spinach leaves, pineapple, capsicum on top of the pizza - get creative!
- Place pizza into the dehydrator for 2-3 hours at 115F/ 46C
- Serve straight from the dehydrator warm!

Lettuce Boats

serves 2-4

Ingredients

- 1 cup of walnuts or sunflower seeds
- 1 cup of mushrooms
- 1 Tablespoon of linseed oil
- 1 Tablespoon of cumin powder
- 2 teaspoons of coriander powder
- A pinch of Himalayan sea salt

Method

- Place all ingredients into a food processor and process into small pieces - ensuring the mixture has texture.
- Place mixture into lettuce leaf cups and sprinkle with raw vegetables of your choice, such as chopped tomato, sliced avocado, grated carrot and cubes of cucumber.
- Drizzle with tahini cream (see page 97)

Raw Pasta

serves 2-4

Ingredients

Noodles: 4-6 medium zucchinis . You will need a spiraliser for this recipe.

Pasta sauce:
- 4-5 tomatoes
- 1 cup of sun-dried tomatoes
- 1 teaspoon of Himalayan sea salt
- 2 Tablespoons of nama shoyu
- 1 brown onion
- 1 teaspoon of dried basil
- 4 dates pitted
- 1 teaspoon of nutritional yeast
- 1 small clove of garlic
- 1/3 cup of cashews

Method

- To make the noddles cut one end off the zucchini and spiralise as per instructions.
- Place all pasta sauce ingredients into a high powered blender until the sauce is creamy!
- Pour sauce on top of the noddles and stir through! It is so quick and easy and kids just love the spiral noodles!

kids salad serves 2

ingredients

- 1 mango
- 1/2 avocado
- 1 tomato
- 1 cup of organic corn
- 1 cup of cubed cucumber
- 1 cup of grated carrot
- 1 cup of lettuce *Optional a lot of young children do not like the texture of lettuce.

Method

- Mix all the ingredients together in bowl.
- Drizzle with tahini cream or a simple apple cider vinegar dressing.

Raw snacks...

Issy's Kale Chips

Apple Muffins

Mesquite Balls

Chocolate Chia Balls

Apricot Balls

Teddy Bear Biscuits

Fruit Roll Ups

Sweet Potato Chips

Apple Goji Bars

Apple Cookies

Muesli Bars

All Seed Bar

ISSY'S KALE CHIPS

Fills 4 Excalibur trays

Ingredients

- 2 large bunches of organic kale
- 1 1/2 cups of raw cashews
- Juice of one lemon or half an orange
- 1 Tablespoon of miso paste
- 1/4 cup of nama shoyu
- 1 Tablespoon of tahini
- 1 teaspoon of Himalayan sea salt
- 3/4 cup of water

Method

- Remove kale leaves from the stems of the kale and tear up into small pieces, placing them in a bowl.
- Place sauce ingredients in a high powered blender adding water until smooth.
- Massage the sauce into the kale and place on paraflex sheets.
- Dehydrate for 6-8 hours at 115F/46C until crunchy.
- And there you have it beautiful yummy crunchy raw kale chips.
- Will keep in a sealed container for up to two weeks!

Raw Apple Muffins

Makes 8-12 muffins

Ingredients

- 1 cup of buckwheat
- 1/2 cup of ground flax seeds
- 1/4 cup of mesquite powder
- 3/4 cup of water
- 1 Tablespoon of linseed oil
- 4 apples peeled and cored
- 1/2 Tablespoon of cinnamon
- A pinch of Himalayan sea salt

Method

- Soak buckwheat for 12 hours, rinse and drain.
- Mix the ground flax seeds, buckwheat, mesquite powder, cinnamon and salt in a large mixing bowl.
- Puree apples. Place half of the apple puree aside.
- Place the other half of the apple puree in with dry ingredients with water and stir until smooth.
- Place a small amount of mixture in a cup cake pattie and then create a hole with you finger, place a small amount of the remaining apple puree in the hole, then cover with remaining muffin mixture.
- Dehydrate for six hours at 115F/46C – then remove from cases and dehydrate for a further four hours.
- These are delicious with some fresh berries or raw honey and will keep for four days in a sealed container in the fridge.

Chocolate Chia Balls

Makes 20-26 balls

Ingredients

- 4 cups of walnuts
- 1 cup of soaked goji berries
- 1/4 cup of chia seeds
- 1 cup of organic sultanas
- 1/2 cup of dried organic apricots
- 1/4 cup of dates pitted
- 1/4 cup of desiccated coconut
- 4 Tablespoons of carob powder
- 4 Tablespoons of coconut nectar or 2 drops of stevia (flavoured or plain)

Method

- Mix all dry ingredients together in a food processor until combined.
- Adding sweetener at the end to bind.
- Roll into balls and cover in excess coconut.
- Store in a sealed container in the freezer.

apricot balls

makes 12-16 balls

ingredients

- 1 cup of almonds
- 1 cup of shredded coconut
- 2 cups of organic dried apricots
- Juice of 1 orange
- 1 Tablespoon of grated orange rind

Method

- Grind almonds in a food processor until fine, add remaining ingredients until well mixed.
- Roll into little balls and coat with excess coconut.
- These would also be nice with a little raw cacao nibs for the chocolate lovers out there.
- Store in a sealed container in the freezer.

mesquite balls

Makes 10-12 balls

ingredients

- 1 cup of walnuts
- 1/4 cup of carob powder
- 1/4 cup of mesquite powder
- 1/4 cup of soaked goji berries
- 4 soaked dates pitted
- 1/2 cup of organic sultanas

Method

- Pulse nuts in food processor until crumb like.
- Add carob and mesquite powders then add sultanas, drained goji berries and dates until well mixed.
- Roll into balls, coating with mesquite powder.
- Store in a sealed container in the freezer.

Teething RUSKS

Makes 18-20 teething RUSKS

ingredients

- 1/2 cup of ground flax seeds
- 1 cup of mesquite powder
- 1 cup of raw almonds
- 1/2 cup of goji berries
- 3 apples peeled and cored
- 6 organic apricots
- 1 cup of water (add more if required)

Method

- Blend almonds in a food processor until flour like.
- Add remaining ingredients and process until finely ground.
- You can use a piping bag to create logs, or you can spread mixture on paraflex sheets and mark bars using a knife.
- Dehydrate at 145F/46C for one hour flip then reduce to 115F/46C for a further 6 hours.

Teddy Bear Biscuits Makes 8-10

Ingredients

- 1 cup of raw cashews
- 1 cup of coconut flakes
- Juice of one lemon
- 1 Tablespoon of coconut nectar

Method

- Process cashews and coconut in a food processor, until mixture is fine.
- Add lemon and coconut nectar and process.
- Form squares on paraflex sheets that are big enough for your teddy bear biscuit cutters. Repeat until you have used all the mixture up.
- Dehydrate on 115F /46C degrees for 6 hours, then flip and dehydrate for another 1 -2 hours.

FRUIT ROLL UPS

Method

- Puree fruit of choice using a high powered blender until completely smooth, making sure there are no lumps left, not even little ones.

- Grease dehydrator paraflex sheet with a thin layer of coconut oil and pour fruit mixture, using a spatula to make sure it's spread evenly.

- Dehydrate at 115F/46C for 2-3 hours, then flip and dehydrate for further 1-2 hours.

- Fruit leathers should be pliable, but not sticky. Cut into eight equal strips, and roll into cylinder shapes.

- If you find the roll ups to be a bit tart you can add a dash of sweetener like stevia, dates or coconut nectar.

Combinations...

- Strawberry and apple
- Strawberry and banana
- Mango
- Mango and apple
- Peach and apple
- Pear and apple

- Plum, apple and banana
- Apricot, apple and Banana
- Mango and coconut
- Apricot and coconut
- Blueberry and banana
- Mixed berries

sweet potato chips

Fills 2-3 Excalibur trays

ingredients

- 2 large sweet potatoes
- 2 teaspoon of Himalayan sea salt
- 2 Tablespoons of linseed oil

Method

- Peel and slice sweet potatoes as thin as possible using a mandoline.
- Sprinkle, oil salt over the top and massage to distribute evenly.
- Set slices in a single layer on a dehydrator sheet and dehydrate at 115F/46C for 12 hours or until nice and crispy.
- Will keep in a sealed container for up to two weeks.

apple goji bars makes 18-20 bars

ingredients

- 1 1/2 cups of buckwheat
- 1/2 cup of mesquite powder
- 2 organic apples chopped finely
- 1/2 cup of soaked goji berries
- 1/2 cup of ground flax seeds
- 1/2 teaspoon of vanilla extract
- A pinch of Himalayan sea salt

Method

- Soak buckwheat overnight, rinse and drain.
- Blend buckwheat in a high powered blender until it becomes a paste, you may need to add water to get it going.
- Place all the ingredients in a mixing bowl and mix. You may need to add a little water, but it should be a dough consistency once mixed.
- Spread mixture onto dehydrator sheets until you form a square.
- Cut into bar shapes.
- Dehydrate at 115F/46C for 4-5 hours. Then split the bars where the cut marks are and flip bars and dehydrate for a further 3-4 hours.

Apple Cookies

makes 10 - 12

Ingredients

- 6 apples peeled and cored
- 1 cup of ground almonds
- 1 cup of organic sultanas
- 3 Tablespoons of cinnamon
- 1 cup of mesquite powder
- 3/4 cup of coconut nectar

Method

- In a food processor shred the apples or chop finely by hand.
- Place all remaining ingredients into a mixing bowl and mix well.
- Form small cookie sizes and place onto paraflex sheets.
- Dehydrator at 115F/46C for 12-16 hours
- These cookies will take a little while to crunch up.

Muesli Balls

makes 14 - 16

Ingredients

- 2 cups of buckwheat
- 1/2 cup of sunflower seeds
- 1 Tablespoon of chia seeds
- 1/2 cup of shredded coconut
- 1 cup of pitted dates
- 1/2 cup of organic sultanas
- 1 cup of organic blueberries
- 1/4 cup of coconut nectar
- 1 teaspoon of vanilla extract
- 1 teaspoon of cinnamon

Method

- Soak buckwheat for 12 hours, rinse and drain.
- Place one cup of buckwheat into the blender with dates, agave, and vanilla. Blend until smooth. Place sunflower seeds and remaining cup of buckwheat and pulse just enough so that it is blended with texture but not smooth. You could also do this using a food processor.
- Place all remaining ingredients into a bowl and fold, mixing gently.
- Place mixture onto paraflex sheet creating a rectangle.
- Place into dehydrator at 115F/46C for 4 hours. Then mark into bars using a sharp knife.
- Dehydrate for another 12 hours or until nice and crunchy.

ALL SEED BAR

makes 16-20

ingredients

- 1/2 cup of sunflower seeds
- 1/2 cup of sesame seeds
- 1/2 cup of soaked flaxseeds
- 1/2 cup of pepitas
- 1/2 cup of chopped raw almonds
- 1/2 cup of raw honey
- 1/2 cup of tahini
- 1/4 cup of coconut oil

Method

- Place all seeds in a bowl except the almonds.
- Chop almonds finely and then place in the bowl - mixing all ingredients well.
- Pour tahini, honey and melted coconut oil over nut mixture stirring until it becomes sticky.
- Press into a baking tray and mark bars with a knife and place into the freezer to set.
- Try adding sultanas, goji berries, apricots and other fruits to spice up this great seed bar!

CRACKeRS & BReAd...

honey buns

veggie crackers

raw bread

banana bread

sun-dried tomato & olive bread

savoury bread

flaxseed crackers

zucchini wraps

coconut wraps

HONEY BUNS

makes 6-8 rolls

ingredients

- 1 cup of raw almonds
- 1 cup of buckwheat
- 3/4 cup of ground linseeds
- 1 cup of psyllium husk
- 1 teaspoon of Himalayan sea salt
- 2 cups of filtered water
- Juice of two lemons

Method

- Soak buckwheat for 1 hour.
- Place almonds and buckwheat into the food processor and process until fine.
- Place flour and remaining dry ingredients into a bowl adding liquid ingredients mixing until dough like.
- Form into small buns and place into the dehydrator at 145F/62C for 1 hour then reduce temp to 115F/46C for remaining 6-8 hours.
- Best stored in the fridge and will last 2-3 days.

Veggie Crackers

Fills 4 excalibur trays

Ingredients

- 3 cups of flax seeds
- 1 cup of chia seeds
- 2 cups of raw almonds
- 2 cups of grated carrot
- 1 cup of fresh parsley
- 1/2 cup of sesame seeds
- 1/2 cup of pumpkin seeds
- Juice of 2 lemons
- 2 teaspoons of Himalayan sea salt
- 2 teaspoons of kelp powder (optional)

Method

- Soak chia seeds, flax seeds and almonds over night. Remove the skins from the almonds after soaking.
- Place chia, flax and almonds in a food processor and process until crumb like. Add carrots, sesame seeds and pumpkin seeds, salt and juice of lemon and pulse mixture until well blended.
- Place mixture onto paraflex sheets, filling mixture to the edge.
- Dehydrate at 115F/46C degrees for 2- 3 hours, then score into squares.
- Dehydrate for a further 10-12 hours at 115F/46C.
- Will store up to 3 weeks in an air tight container.

Raw Bread

Makes 1 large loaf

Ingredients

- 7 cups of almond pulp (save the almond pulp from making nut milk by placing it in the freezer to keep. Simply defrost when making raw bread)
- 6 drops of hazelnut stevia – it gives a nice nutty flavor (you can also you plain stevia)
- 1/2 tablespoon of salt
- 1/2 cup of ground linseed's
- 1/2 cup of olive oil

Method

- Place all ingredients apart from the oil and linseed's into a large bowl and mix thoroughly
- Add a little of the oil and linseed's at a time whilst kneading into a dough (linseed's will absorb the moisture and expand) – keep adding a little oil and little linseed's at time and knead again – repeat until all the oil and linseed's have been used.
- Shape the dough into a loaf and place on a chopping board which has been lined with ground linseed's so the dough doesn't stick.
- Cut into bread slices and place on excalibur mesh trays.
- Dehydrate at 115F/46C for 3 hours.
- Best stored in the fridge and will store for 2-3 days.

Savoury Bread

Makes 2 small loaves

Ingredients

- 2 cups of raw almonds or almond pulp
- 1/2 cup of cauliflower
- 1 cup of psyllium husk
- 2 cloves of garlic
- 1 cup of chopped brown onion
- 1/2 cup of ground flax seeds
- 1 Tablespoon of nutritional yeast
- 1 teaspoon of Himalayan sea salt
- Juice of half a lemon
- 1 1/2 cups of filtered water

Method

- Process almonds with a food processor until flour like, then add cauliflower processing until mixed.
- Place flour and remaining dry ingredients into a bowl and mix well.
- Add remaining liquid ingredients stirring until dough like.
- Separate the mixture in half forming two small loaf shapes.
- Shape the dough into a loaf and place on a chopping board which has been lined with ground linseed's so the dough doesn't stick.
- Cut into bread slices and place on excalibur mesh trays.
- Dehydrate at 115F/46C for 3 hours.
- Best stored in the fridge and will store for 2-3 days.

Banana Bread

Makes 2 small loaves

Ingredients

- 2 mashed bananas
- 1 cup of raw almonds or almond pulp
- 1 cup of psyllium husk
- 1 cup of walnuts chopped finely
- 1/2 cup of ground flax seeds
- 1 teaspoon of mesquite powder
- 1/2 cup chopped dates
- 1 teaspoon of Himalayan sea salt
- 1 cup of filtered water (you may need to add more)

Method

- Mash bananas in a bowl and set aside.
- Process almonds in a food processor until flour like.
- Place flour and remaining dry ingredients into a bowl and mix well.
- Add mashed banana and remaining liquid ingredients mixing until dough like.
- Form two small loaf shapes and place into the dehydrator at 145F/46C for 1 hour then reduce temp to 115F/46C for 10-12 hours.
- Best stored in the fridge and will last 2-3 days.

Sun-dried Tomato & Olive Bread
Makes 2 small loaves

Ingredients

- 2 cups of raw almonds
- 1 cup of psyllium husk
- 1/2 cup of ground flax seeds
- 1/4 cup of chopped olives
- 1/4 cup of chopped sun-dried tomatoes
- 2 cloves garlic
- 1 cup of chopped brown onion
- 1 Tablespoon of mixed Italian herbs
- 1 teaspoon of salt
- Juice of half a lemon
- 1 1/2 cup of filtered water and more if necessary

Method

- Process almonds with a food processor until flour like.
- Place flour and remaining dry ingredients into a bowl and mix well.
- Add remaining liquid ingredients until dough like.
- Shape the dough into a loaf and place on a chopping board which has been lined with ground linseed's so the dough doesn't stick.
- Cut into bread slices and place on excalibur mesh trays.
- Dehydrate at 115F/46C for 3 hours.
- Best stored in the fridge and will store for 2-3 days.

Banana Crackers

fills 2 Excalibur trays

Ingredients

- 1 cup of flaxseeds
- 1 cup of ground flaxseed
- 1/2 cup of chia seeds
- 3 ripe bananas mashed
- 1/2 cup of finely chopped walnuts
- Pinch of Himalayan sea salt

Method

- Soak flaxseeds for a minimum of 8 hours, rinse and drain.
- Place the flaxseeds, ground flaxseeds, chia seeds, bananas and nuts into a bowl and mix well.
- Place mixture onto paraflex sheets filling to the edge.
- Dehydrator at 115F/46C for 2 hours.
- Score the crackers into square shapes and flip over and dehydrate for another 4 hours at 115F/46C until crunchy.

FLAXSEED BREAD

fills 4 excalibur trays

ingredients

- 2 cups of ground flax seeds
- 1 1/3 cup of sunflower seeds
- 1/2 cup of sesame seeds
- 1 teaspoon of Himalayan sea salt
- 1 clove of minced garlic
- 1 brown onion chopped finely
- 1/4 cup of nama shoyu
- 1 3/4 cup of water

Method

- Place all dry ingredients into a bowl and mix until combined.
- Add nama shoyu and water starting with 1 cup and then slowly add the remaining 1 cup of water until there is thick consistency in the mixture.
- You should be able to easily spread this onto paraflex trays - filling the trays to the edge.
- Dehydrator at 115F/46C for 4 hours. Cut each tray into 4 quarters.
- Flip and dehydrate for another 2-3 hours at 115F/46C.
- Refrigerate and store in a air tight container for 6-7 days.

zucchini wraps

makes 4

ingredients

- 4-5 medium zucchinis
- 2 cups of ground flax seeds
- Pinch of Himalayan sea salt

Method

- Place zucchini and ground flax seeds into high powered blender until smooth.
- Add a pinch of salt and a little water if needed, there should be enough water in the zucchinis.
- Place mixture onto paraflex sheets forming circles.
- Dehydrate at 115F/46C for one hour.
- This is where you need to keep checking on your wraps, as they can easily turn into thin crackers.
- Further dehydrate for 2-3 hours.
- They need to be pliable and easy to role. When making wraps I suggest doing it on a day that your home so you check on the dehydration process before they turn to veggie chips!

coconut wraps

makes 4

ingredients

- Meat from 4 young coconuts
- 1/4 cup of water or coconut water
- 4 Tablespoons of ground flax seeds
- A pinch of Himalayan sea salt

Method

- Place all ingredients into a high powered blender until completely smooth - no lumps!
- Place mixture onto paraflex sheets forming circles.
- Dehydrate at 115F/46C for one hour.
- This is where you need to keep checking on your wraps, as they can easily turn into thin crackers.
- Further dehydrate for 2-3 hours.
- They should be able to easily roll of the paraflex sheets.

Milk, Butter & Yoghurt...

Almond butter

Almond milk

Sunflower milk

Coconut yoghurt

ALMONd BUTTER

ingredients

- 2 cups of raw almonds
- 2 Tablespoons of linseed oil or olive oil

Method

- Process almonds with an S blade in food processor for 10 minutes.
- You will need to start scrapping down the sides in the beginning.
- As the oils are released from the almonds, they will start to stick together and form a large mass that moves around the bowl.
- Keep processing for a further 20-25 minutes, the oils from the almonds are further released and a nut butter type texture will start forming.
- Add the linseed oil and mix further then jar and refrigerate.

TIPS to making almond butter

- Do not use soaked almonds, without thoroughly drying them in the dehydrator.
- Do not add any liquid until the end as it is best that the natural oils are realised first.
- Ensure you store your almond butter in a sealed jar in the fridge.

Almond Milk

Almond milk contains more nutrients than other dairy milk alternatives like rice milk. The health benefits provided by this option even match dairy choices.

Almond milk works as a great alternative for those with soy and lactose allergies. Almond milk also contains 30% of our recommended daily value of calcium and 25% of vitamin D, for strong bones in

Soaking Almonds

When making almond milk it is important to soak the almonds for at least 8 hours. Almond milk is much creamier when the skins are removed, however a nut milk bag will also help catch almond skins.

How to Peel Almonds

The outer shell or skin of the almonds contain lectins which we can not digest. By soaking and peeling almonds you remove the lectins and the body is therefore able to digest the almonds.

1. Soak almonds overnight or for 6-8 hours.
2. Bring a large pot of water to the boil or simply boil kettle.
3. Add your raw almonds – skin on into the hot water.
4. Allow almonds to be submerged for about 30-60 seconds.
5. Remove almonds and drain away water.
6. Press each almond between your fingers to "pop" the almond out of the shell.

Ingredients

- 1 cup of raw almonds
- 4 cups of filtered water
- You can add a sweetener if desired; try honey, dates, cinnamon or vanilla extract.

Method

- Soak almonds for 8 hours and remove skins (as per instructions)
- Place almonds in your blender with the 4 cups of filtered water and blend until nice and creamy.
- You can either use a nut bag or a sieve.
- Drain milk leaving the almond pulp behind.
- Use straight away or refrigerate in a sealed container.
- Almond milk will keep in the fridge for 2-3 days.

What do you do with the almond pulp?

- Left over almond pulp can be used as almond flour.
- Simply feeze the almond pulp by placing it in a zip lock bag in the freezer and defrost as needed.

sunflower milk

Sunflower seeds are an incredibly rich source of calcium, iron, manganese, zinc, magnesium, selenium, and copper. Many of these minerals play a vital role in bone materialization, red blood cell production, enzyme synthesis, hormone production and help regulation of cardiac and skeletal muscle activities.

Sunflower milk has a unique flavour so a little natural sweetener will ensure your kids keep coming back for more.

ingredients

- 1 cup of soaked sunflower seeds
- 3 cups of filtered water or more to taste
- 1 teaspoon of vanilla extract
- 3 pitted dates
- A pinch of Himalayan sea salt

Method

- As per almond milk

Try adding some mesquite or vanilla as it gives a great taste to nut and seed milk!

Coconut Yoghurt

Ingredients

- Meat of 2 young coconuts
- 1 teaspoon of pro-biotic

Method

- Place the meat of two young coconuts into a high powered blender and blend until smooth. You may need to add a little coconut water to get it going, then add the pro-biotic powder until well mixed.
- Pour mixture into a jar, leaving some room at the top as yoghurt will aerate as it cultures.
- Place a lid on the jar and leave in a warmish place, covering with a tea towel and let it sit to culture for 8-12 hours.
- You will know when your coconut yoghurt is ready when bubbles have formed throughout the yoghurt.
- You can then add flavours such as vanilla, cinnamon and honey.
- Coconut yoghurt will last 5 - 7 days when stored in a sealed container and refrigerated.

Cheese & Creams...

RAW Cheese

Cheese sticks

Tahini cream

Nut cream

Sunflower dip

RAW Cheese

Ingredients

- 2 cups of macadamia nuts

or;

- 1 cup of macadamia nuts and 1 cup of cashews
- 1 cup of water
- 1 teaspoon of probiotics
- 2 Tablespoons of nutritional yeast

Method

- Blend nuts, water and probiotics in a high powered blender until smooth, ensuring there are no lumps.

- Place a cheese cloth on top of a sieve, then poor mixture into the cheese cloth, fold cheese cloth over the top of the cheese mixture - making sure there is a container placed underneath to catch the excess liquid.

- Place a weight on the top of the cheese cloth - this will help push the excess water out from the cheese. A jar filled with water will suffice.

- Cover the jar and weight with a tea towel and leave at room temp for 24 hours.

- After 24 hours remove the cheese mixture from the cheese cloth and place into a bowl mixing in a pinch of salt, squeeze of lemon and 2 tablespoons of nutritional yeast.

- Place cheese in a round ring pushing the mixture out to form the cheese shape. Dehydrate at 115F/46C for 12 hours to create a rind if desired.

- Store refrigerated, will keep for 7 days.

Cheese hemp sticks

ingredients

- 4 cups of sunflower seeds
- 1/2 cup of lemon juice
- 1/2 cup of namu shoyu
- 4 cloves of garlic
- 3 teaspoon of nutritional yeast
- 1 teaspoon of hemp seeds

Method

- Grind the sunflower seeds in a food processor until crumb like.
- Add lemon juice, namu shoyu and nutritional yeast until sticky.
- Create cheese sticks shapes and coat with hemp seeds.
- Place onto paraflex sheets.
- Dehydrate at 115F/46C for 12-16 hours.
- Store refrigerated for up to 7 days.

CReam

Tahini CReam

ingRedients

- 1/4 cup of tahini
- 3/4 cup of almond milk
- 3 Tablespoons of raw honey
- 1 teaspoon vanilla extract

Method

- Place all ingredients in a high powered blender and blend until smooth.
- You can use this straight away or place in the refrigerator to thicken.

Nut CReam

ingRedients

- 1 cup of nuts of choice
- 6 pitted dates soaked in 1 cup of water
- 1 teaspoon of vanilla extract

Method

- Place all ingredients in a high powered blender and blend until smooth.
- You can use this straight away or place in the refrigerator to thicken.

sunflower dip

ingredients

- 1/2 cup of sunflower seeds
- 1/4 cup of tahini
- 1/4 cup of water
- Juice of one lemon
- Pinch of Himalayan sea salt

- Optional * 1 x garlic clove

Method

- Place all ingredients into a high powered blender until smooth.
- You can use this straight away or place in the refrigerator to thicken.
- This dip is great served with raw crackers or vegetable sticks.

Sweets & Treats...

Banana Muffins

Banana Cream

Ice Cream & Toppings

Ice Cream & Toppings

Chocolate Mousse

Mini Cheesecakes

Chocolate Brownies

Chocolate Crackles

Raw Chocolate

Juice Cake

Banana Muffins  makes 10-12

Ingredients

- 3 bananas
- 1 cup of raw almonds
- 1/2 cup of walnuts
- 4 pitted dates soaked in 1/4 cup of water
- 1 - 2 Tablespoons of raw honey
- 1 teaspoon vanilla extract
- 2 teaspoons of cinnamon

Method

- Mash the bananas in a bowl and set aside.
- Combine walnuts, almonds in a food processor and combine until flour like.
- Add soaked dates, water, honey, vanilla and cinnamon and process.
- Place all ingredients into a bowl and mix in mashed bananas.
- Place mixture into muffin cups.
- Dehydrate for 1 hour at 145F/62C then reduce to 115F/46 for 10 -12 hours
- Top muffins with banana cream and refrigerate for an hour or until cream sets.

Banana Cream

Ingredients

- 1 cup of soaked raw cashews
- 1 banana
- Squeeze of half a lemon
- 1 teaspoon of vanilla extract
- 2 Tablespoons of coconut oil
- 2 Tablespoons of sweetener of choice honey or coconut nectar (you can even leave out the sweetener out if you like!)

Method

- Soak cashews for 2-3 hours, rinse and drain.
- Place all ingredients in a high powered blender until smooth.
- You may need to add a little water if the cashews get stuck in the blender to get it going until it is completley smooth.
- Place in the fridge for an hour until cream thickens.
- This is a great cream to use with all raw deserts.

ice cream & Toppings

Method

- It is so simple all you need is frozen bananas!

- Slice ripe bananas into chunks and place in a container or plastic bag in the freezer for at least 12- 24 hours or until frozen.

- Place banana chunks in a high powered blender and blend until smooth.

- Add your favourite fruits or superfoods to create yummy and nutritous raw ice-creams.

Flavour your ice cream with...

- Raw cacao, or carob powder
- Raw chocolate coconut butter
- Vanilla bean
- Chopped mint
- Strawberries
- Blueberries
- Chopped almonds
- Raw cacao nibs
- Walnut and honey
- Shredded coconut

Strawberry
Stir in frozen berries or even better fresh!

Chocolate Topping
Raw coconut chocolate butter

Monkey Mango
Fresh mango & chopped macadamia nuts

Coconut Cream
Add 1 Tablespoon of shredded coconut.

Hokey Pokey
Crushed walnuts, with a swirl of raw honey

Chocolate chip
Sprinkle raw cacao nips through banana ice cream

Raw Pop Corn

Ingredients

- 1 whole cauliflower head
- 1 teaspoon of sea salt
- 1/2 cup of nutritional yeast (enough to coat all the cauliflower pieces)
- 1 Tablespoon of coconut oil

Method

- Break the cauliflower florets from the cauliflower or simply cut off with a knife.
- Note when dehydrating the cauliflower it will shrink as the water content is removed, so don't break the cauliflower up too small otherwise you will get cauliflower crumbs not pop corn sizes!
- In a bowl coat the cauliflower with the coconut oil then cover with nutritional yeast (use liberally if you want a cheesy flavour) and salt!
- Place the pop corn pieces onto a mesh sheet and into the dehydrator for 6-8 hours at 115F.
- Raw pop corn is a great snack when watching a movie with the kids or a great snack at children's parties!

Chocolate mousse

serves 2

ingredients

- 1 ripe avocado
- 2 ripe bananas
- 2 frozen bananas
- 1/4 cup of cacao or carob powder
- 3 soaked pitted dates

Method

- Place avocado, bananas, carob powder and dates into a high powered blender until smooth - ensuring there are no lumps.
- Serve straight away or place in the fridge for one hour to thicken.
- Serve with fresh fruit.

Mini Cheese cakes

ingredients

Base

- 2 cups of macadamia nuts
- 1/2 cup of pitted dates
- 1/2 cup of shredded coconut

Filling

- 3 cups of raw cashews soaked for 2 hours
- 1/2 cup of coconut nectar
- 1/2 cup of lemon juice
- 1 teaspoon of Himalayan sea salt
- 1/2 cup of water
- 1/2 cup of coconut oil
- 1/2 cup of berries of choice

Method

- Base: Process macadamia nuts, dates and coconut using a food processor until crumb like, you can add a bit of water to help bind the base if needed.
- Press the mixture into a cake tin where the sides come apart from the base. Or if you want to get creative, you can use cookie cutter shapes but make sure you line the sides with some coconut oil so the cheese cakes can be easily pushed through.
- *For the filling:* Place all ingredients in a high powered blender and blend until completley smooth.
- Pour the filling over the base and place in the freezer for at least two hours to set.
- Place in the fridge to defrost and serve with your favourite fresh berries.

Chocolate Brownies

makes 10-12

ingredients

Base...

- 1 cup of walnuts
- 1 cup of pitted dates
- 1 teaspoon of cinnamon
- 1/2 vanilla bean
- 1 Tablespoon of coconut nectar
- 1/4 cup of desiccated coconut
- 4 Tablespoons of cacao or carob powder

Topping...

- 1/2 avocado
- 2 Tablespoons of carob powder
- 2 Tablespoons of coconut oil
- 1 cup of water
- 4 soaked pitted dates

Method

- To make the base place walnuts in a food processor until crumb like.
- Add remaining base ingredients until sticky.
- Firm mixture into a square tin and place in freezer to set.
- To make the topping place all topping ingredients in a high powered blender until smooth, making sure there are no lumps.
- Poor topping mixture over the base and place into the freezer for at least one hour to set. Score into bar shapes and serve.

Chocolate Crackles

makes 10-12

ingredients

- 1 banana
- 1/4 cup of coconut oil
- 1/4 cup of coconut nectar
- 1/2 teaspoon of vanilla extract
- 1/3 cup of cacao or carob powder
- 2 cups of shredded coconut

Method

- To melt coconut oil, place the coconut oil jar into a bowl of boiling hot water.
- Place melted coconut oil, honey and vanilla into a mixing bowl until smooth.
- Sift in the cocao or carob powder until combined, then stir in shredded coconut.
- Place mixture into cupcakes and place into the freezer for at least an hour to set!
- These are great for kids parties!

Raw Chocolate

Ingredients

- 1/2 cup of coconut oil
- 1/2 cup of almond butter
- 2-3 dates soaked in 1/4 cup of water
- 1/2 cup of carob powder
- 2 drops of flavoured stevia (cherry, strawberry, hazlenut, caramel)
- 1/4 cup of chopped walnuts (optional)

Method

- Over hot water in a double container, place coconut oil, stevia, almond butter and soaked dates and stir until all ingredients are melted and smooth.
- Add in carob power and mix until smooth, then add remaining nuts.
- Pour into chocolate moulds and freeze until set.

Juice Pulp Cake

Ingredients

Cake
- 3 cups of left over juice pulp
- 1/2 cup of ground raw almonds
- 1/2 cup of pitted dates – chopped
- 1/2 cup of psyllium husk
- 1 teaspoon of nutmeg

Lemon date icing
- 1 cup of soaked pitted dates
- Juice of one lemon
- 2 teaspoons of psyllium husk
- Rind of one lemon
- 1-2 tablespoons of coconut nectar

Method

- Place all cake ingredients into a food processor until well mixed.
- Press cake mixture into a cake tin. Make sure the sides can be removed.
- To make the icing: Blend all ingredients in a high powered blender until smooth.
- Pour icing over the cake and refrigerate for 1-2 hours or until set.

RAW RESOURCES...

Pantry Supplies

Substitution Chart

Kitchen Equipment

Conversion Chart

Meal Planner

Raw Food Pantry supplies...

- ☐ **Fresh fruits** - apples, pears, pineapple, banana, apples, pears, oranges and more...
- ☐ **Vegetables** - carrots, turnips, sweet potatoes, parsnips, sweet potato, pumpkin, potatoes, carrots, zucchini and more
- ☐ **Salad vegetables -** cucumber, cherry tomatoes, capsicum, cabbage tomatoes, bell peppers, kale, watercress, chard
- ☐ **Leafy green vegetables -** rocket, baby spinach, beetroot greens, kale
- ☐ **Herbs -** mint, coriander, basil, oregano, parsley, thyme
- ☐ **Nuts -** almonds, pecans, walnuts, pine nuts, cashews, macadamia
- ☐ **Dried fruits** - prunes, raisins, sultanas, apricots, dates, figs, raisins, currants, goji berries
- ☐ **Sprouted legumes & beans -** pulses and legumes, aduki, mung, chickpea, lentil
- ☐ **Sprouted seeds** - quinoa, buckwheat, millet
- ☐ **Sprouted grains -** barley, rye, wheat
- ☐ **Sprouted vegetable seeds -** broccoli, mustard, cress
- ☐ **Seeds** - pumpkin, sesame, sunflower pumpkin, sesame, chia, hemp
- ☐ **Indoor greens** - wheat grass, sunflower greens, pea shoots, sunflower shoots.
- ☐ **Edible flowers** - wild rose petals, honeysuckle, lavender blossoms
- ☐ **Mushrooms** - oyster, portobello, reishi
- ☐ **Sea vegetables** - dulse, wakame, kelp arame, nori
- ☐ **Algaes** - chlorella, spirulina, blue-green algae
- ☐ **Oils** - olive oil, sesame oil, hemp oil, coconut oil, flaxseed oil
- ☐ **Stimulants** - onion, garlic, cayenne pepper
- ☐ **Spices** - cinnamon, turmeric, cumin, nutmeg
- ☐ **Sweeteners** - cacao, honey, mesquite, agave syrup, coconut nectar, stevia
- ☐ **Super foods -** maca, camu camu, cacao, acai, goji, aloe vera, lacuma
- ☐ **Prepackaged/prepared raw foods** - nut butters, seed butters, flax crackers

substitution options...

SUGAR

Bad	Better	Best
Dextrose	Raw agave	Stevia
Corn syrup	Maple syrup	Vanilla
Rice syup	Raisins	Cinnamon
Malt	Coconut sugar	Raw honey
		Dates
		Coconut nectar

sweeteners

Bad	Better	Best
Aspartime	Xylitol	Stevia
Splenda	Coconut sugar	Dates
	coconut nectar	Mesquite

salt

Bad	Better	Best
Table salt	Unrefined sea salt	Organic salt
Iodized salt	Unrefined celtic sea salt	Celery salt
		Himalayan sea salt

FLOUR

Bad	Better	Best
White flours from:	Organic whole flours from	Sprouted grains
Wheat	Spelt	Almond flour
Corn	Kamut	Coconut flour
Rice	Quinoa	Cashew flour
	Brown rice	Buckwheat

BREAD

Bad	Better	Best
Packaged long shelf life bread	Home made	Raw bread
	Sour dough (yeast free)	Flax bread
	Wheat free	Essene bread
White	Sprouted bread	Lettuce wraps
		Zucchini/ Coconut wraps

Pasta

Bad	Better	Best
White pasta	Organic spelt	Raw zucchini pasta
	Buckwheat pasta	
	Spinach pasta	

FATS

Bad	Better	Best
Butter	Olive oil	Cold pressed coconut oil
Margarine		Hemp seed oil
Trans fats		Flaxseed oil
Animal fats		Nuts
		Avocado

Cheese

Bad	Better	Best
Cheese from diary cows	Organic raw goat cheese	Nut cheese
Pasteurized		Seed cheese
Non organic homogenized		

Milk & yoghurt

Bad	Better	Best
Milk from diary cows	Almond milk from store	Nut milk
Pasteurized	Rice milk	Seed milk
Non-organic homogenized	Oat milk	Home made kefir
	Keifr - goats or cows	Coconut milk
		Coconut Yogurt

Kitchen Essentials...

If you are exploring the raw food lifestyle with your family, there a few kitchen items you may want to invest in to make life a little easier!
We stock all of thse items at our online store:
The Raw Food Store - www.therawfoodstore.com.au

High Powered Blender

A high powered blender is a piece of equipment that we use everyday. A smoothie made in a cheaper blender compared to high powered blender creates a very different end product. A high powered blender will create food that is much smoother. It will also last a lot longer.

The Optimum blenders are my blender of choice. The motor is extremely powerful and it will blend ingredients in a matter of seconds. The Optimum blender is also a very affordable option than some of the higher priced blenders on the market.

A Dehydrator

The Excalibur dehydrator is pretty much the staple of our raw food kitchen items. If you are thinking of purchasing a dehydrator you can't go pass the Excalibur dehydrator – These come in 4, 5 and 9 trays. For a family I recommend the larger 5 or 9 tray versions and buy some extra paraflex sheets! You will be able to create crackers, breads and snacks in no time. And most importantly you can be assured the food is raw.

Cold Pressed Juicer

Issy has been having fresh green juice since she was 9 months old. Juicing is a great way for the body to assimilate all the vitamins, enzymes and nutrients from vegetables.

There is only one type of juicer I recommend and that is a cold pressed masticating juicer. A cold pressed juicer slowly grinds the juice and does not involve heat, therefore there less oxidation and more nutrients.

A cold pressed juicer is the only way to go if you want to ensure your family gets the most nutrients per juice. You will also save money on the fruits and vegetables in the long run as they use less vegetables to get more juice.

Food Processor

A food processor is used for things such as breads, bliss balls, pates and crackers. Items that can still have texture to them.

Look around for a high quality food processor as this is one of those items that you get what you pay for.

Nut Milk Bag

Nut milk bags are great for making creamy nut milk. You also end up with a bag full of nut pulp that can also be used as a substitute for flour in other recipes.

Spiriliser

These are great for making 'noodles' or 'spaghetti' out of vegetables such as zucchini and carrots. It can also help make your dishes look fancy without too much effort.

Mandoline

A mandoline will allow you to turn things such as sweet potato into thin slices for yummy raw chips. A mandoline is inexpensive but worth the investment.

A Sharp Knife & a Good Chopping Board

By far the most important equipment you can get is a sharp knife and a good chopping board. We use wooden chopping boards, they are a much more sustainable option than the plastic versions.

Stainless Steel Round Forms

These are fantastic for making raw cheeses, and making any dish look restaurant like in quality.

Cake tins & cup cakes

Cake tins are a must for raw cakes! For cupcakes I currently use the re-usable silicone cup-cakes. I ask people to leave the cup cake shells behind, so we can wash and re-use again! They are also suitable for using in dehydrators.

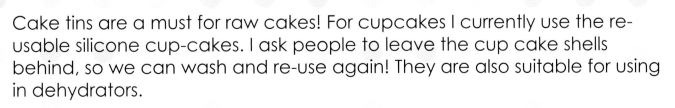

Meal Planner

	Monday	Tuesday	Wednesday
Breakfast			
Lunch			
Dinner			
Snacks			

Thursday	Friday	Saturday	Sunday

conversion charts...

conversion cup > grams > ml

Standard Cup	Fine Powder	Grain	Granular	Liquid Solids	Liquid
1	140g	150 g	190 g	200 g	240 ml
3/4	105 g	113 g	143 g	150 g	180 ml
2/3	93 g	100 g	125 g	133 g	160 ml
1/2	70 g	75 g	95 g	100 g	120 ml
1/3	47 g	50 g	63 g	67 g	80 ml
1/4	35 g	38 g	48 g	50 g	60 ml
1/8	18 g	19 g	24 g	25 g	30 ml

conversion tsp > Tbs > cup > oz > ml

1/4 tsp	-	-	-	1 ml
1/2 tsp	-	-	-	2 ml
1tsp	-	-	-	5 ml
3tsp	1 Tablespoon	-	1/2 fl oz	15 ml
-	2 Tablespoons	1/8 cup	1 fl oz	30 ml
-	4 Tablespoons	1/4 cup	2 fl oz	60 ml
-	5. 1/2 Tablespoon	1/3 cup	3 fl oz	80 ml
-	8 Tablespoon	1/2 cup	4 fl oz	120 ml
-	10. 1/2 Tablespoons	2/3 cup	5 fl oz	160 ml
-	12 Tablespoons	3/4 cup	6 fl oz	180 ml
-	16 Tablespoons	1 cup	8 fl oz	240 ml

About The Raw Food Mum

The Raw Food mum is Sarah (Nolan) Quinney a mum passionate about the health benefits of raw food for children and the whole family.

Sarah is based in Victoria, Australia on the Surf Coast, living with her raw food loving family enjoying the beach and surfing lifestyle.

With over four years experience of eating a raw diet, Sarah knows first hand the benefits and how easy it is to incorporate raw into a family's diet.

If you want learn more about a raw food diet and get Sarah's free recipes don't forget to sign-up for The Raw Food Mums Newsletter – you will love the free quick and delicious recipes designed for the whole family to enjoy.

Check out The Raw Food Mums latest events, programs as well as raw food and organic products at her popular online store The Raw Food Store - www.therawfoodstore.com.au.

the Raw food mum

A raw food loving all things green mum & Store...

The Raw Food Store

Raw. Eco & Sustainable products for the whole family

RAW FOOD

RAW + ORGANIC...

BLENDERS

SPIRALISERS

MASON JARS

GREENS

SUPER GREENS...

SUPER FOODS

RAW + ORGANIC...

www.TheRawFoodStore.com.au
We Ship Across Australia & Internationally